**W9-CPB-784**

DATE DUE JAN 2014

WITHDRAWN

EDGE BOOKS™

TINY CREEPY Creatures

Body Bugs

INVISIBLE CREATURES LURKING INSIDE YOU

by Jennifer Swanson

CONSULTANT:
DEBORAH PHILLIPS, DOCTOR OF EDUCATION
LECTURER, DEPARTMENT OF MICROBIOLOGY
MIAMI UNIVERSITY, OXFORD, OHIO

CAPSTONE PRESS
a capstone imprint

Edge Books are published by Capstone Press,
151 Good Counsel Drive, P.O. Box 669, Mankato, Minnesota 56002.
www.capstonepub.com

 Books published by Capstone Press are manufactured with paper
containing at least 10 percent post-consumer waste.

Library of Congress Cataloging-in-Publication Data
Swanson, Jennifer.
 Body bugs : invisible creatures lurking inside you / by Jennifer Swanson.
   p. cm. — (Edge books. Tiny creepy creatures)
 Includes bibliographical references and index.
 Summary: "Describes microbes commonly found on the human body"—Provided
by publisher.
 ISBN 978-1-4296-6530-8 (library binding)
 ISBN 978-1-4296-7271-9 (paperback)
 1. Microorganisms—Juvenile literature. 2. Bacteria—Juvenile literature. I. Title.
II. Series.

 QR57.S93 2012
 616.9'041—dc22

                                                    2011001981

Editorial Credits

Kristen Mohn, editor; Veronica Correia, designer; Svetlana Zhurkin, media
   researcher; Eric Manske, production specialist

Photo Credits

Alamy: Dattatreya, 25, Medical-on-Line, 8 (bottom), Phototake, 5 (top), 18 (right);
Capstone Studio: Karon Dubke, 18 (left), 21 (bottom), 28; CDC, 19 (bottom left),
22, 26, James Gathany, 23, Janice Haney Carr, cover (bottom), 20; Getty Images:
3D Clinic, 7 (left), G. Wanner, 12 (top), Veronika Burmeister, 16; iStockphoto:
Kansas State University, photo by S.J. Upton, 14 (bottom); Michael Krinke, 29;
Shutterstock: 3445128471, 5 (bottom), carroteater, 27, Dawid Zagorski, 7 (right),
Dhoxax, 12 (bottom), filmfoto, 13 (top), Jiri Hera, 24, Joao Virissimo, 21 (top),
Kai Wong, 13 (bottom), Kokhanchikov, 8 (top), Monkey Business Images, cover
(top), 1, Oleksiy Fedorov, back cover and background throughout, Sebastian
Kaulitzki, 11 (inset), 17, 19 (back), Suzanne Tucker, 14 (top), Vitaly Titov & Maria
Sidelnikova, 15; Svetlana Zhurkin, 11 (back); Visuals Unlimited/Mediscan, 9

Printed in the United States of America in Stevens Point, Wisconsin.
032011   006111WZF11

Table of Contents

Introduction

MEET YOUR MICROBES

A tiny eight-legged insect creeps across a rough, dry surface. A round creature covered with spikes hides in the dark. Slimy, white worms slither along a path covered with acid. Scaly red mounds sprout in moist, warm holes. What is this place? A strange planet? Nope. It's your body.

Your body is home to more than 90 trillion **microbes**. They're on your skin, in your nose, and especially in your stomach and intestines. These microscopic critters are impossible to see with the naked eye, but they are there.

microbe—a living thing that is too small to see without a microscope

tooth bacteria

You have bugs. Everyone does. You might not even know they exist. That's because most microbes don't harm you. Some even help you. Let's zoom in for a closer look.

Chapter 1

THE SKIN YOU'RE IN

Slide your hand along your arm. Feel any microbes? Of course not. But they're there. In fact, your skin is home to billions of bacteria. That doesn't include all the other tiny creatures that might live there, like mites.

Compared to the rest of your body, your skin is rough and dry. It takes a special kind of microbe to live in these conditions. Bacteria are those special bugs.

Bacteria are ancient single-celled life-forms that have lived on Earth for millions or even billions of years. And there are millions of different types of bacteria around.

While being covered in bacteria may sound gross, it is actually normal. Take for example *P. acnes*. These bacteria live in the pores of your skin. They love hiding in the small, dark spaces next to your oil glands. What a great place for a quick snack. Unfortunately, they sometimes cause tiny infections in the skin. We know these as pimples.

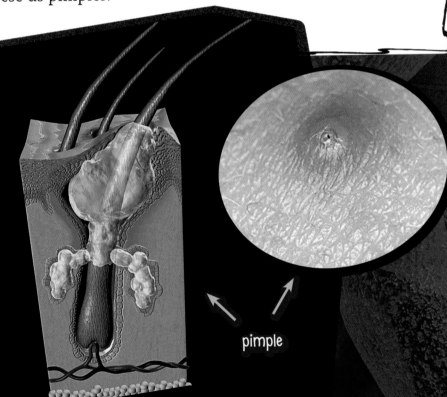

pimple

Ewww Fact!

Did you know that the bacteria living on your skin can be used to identify you? You have your own special bacterial mix unlike anyone else's.

DON'T BLINK

Bacteria aren't the only **organisms** found on your skin. Tiny *demodex* mites live harmlessly in the roots of most people's eyelashes. They feast on oil and dead skin found there. Even the cleanest of people can get these mites. They aren't harmful unless too many of them cling to one eyelash. That may cause redness and irritation. A doctor can provide an ointment to clear it up.

demodex mite

organism—a living thing such as a plant, animal, bacterium, or fungus

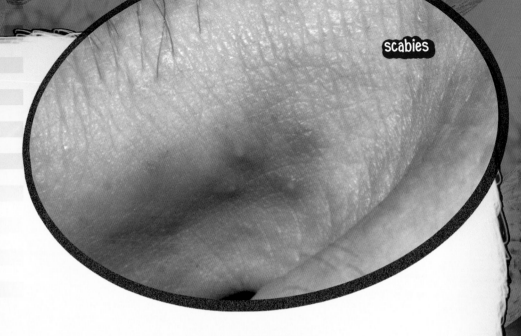

IT MAY BE SCABIES

Scabies mites, or human itch mites, are microscopic animals that can also make your skin their home. Only 0.02 inch (0.5 millimeter) wide, they are slightly bigger than the head of a pin. These eight-legged relatives of spiders are also **parasites**. They feed off the top layer of your skin. Ick!

Tiny female mites can burrow under your skin to lay their eggs. The tunnels they form cause a rash and intense itching. But don't scratch! That will only make it worse. A doctor can provide creams and medicines to kill the mites and stop the itch. Luckily, scabies is not very common. To avoid getting it, be sure to wash your hands often.

parasite—a small organism that lives on or inside a person or animal and causes harm

Chapter 2
THE HOLES IN YOUR HEAD

The nose's job is to act as a filter for the lungs. It does this by using tiny hairs that line its sides. A coating of mucus on the hairs traps dirt, dust, and germs. Don't worry, the gunk doesn't stay there. You'll sneeze or blow it out later.

Even with the filter, some invaders still get in. To a microscopic **virus**, the hair in your nose is like a forest of trees—a great place to hide!

Many viruses are airborne, which means they can enter your nose when you breathe. Round and spiky, long and skinny, or shaped like a spear, viruses work hard to stay put. They find a healthy cell and set up house in it. Then they start infecting other cells.

Luckily, your body can fight off many viruses and get them out of your body. But in the meantime, you might feel sick.

When the mucus in your nose traps dirt or other foreign objects, it makes boogers. But don't pick them! Always use a tissue to avoid putting more germs in your nose.

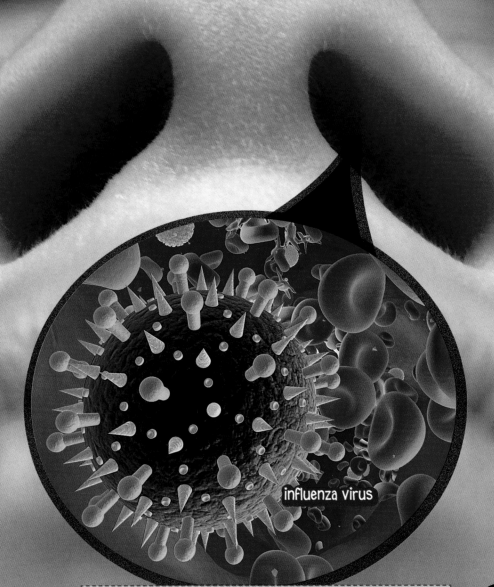

influenza virus

virus—a germ that copies itself inside the body's cells

TEETH CREATURES

Your mouth is a great place to find microbes. More than 500 different types of bacteria live there. Unlike your nose that keeps stuff out, you invite things into your mouth when you eat.

plaque with bacteria

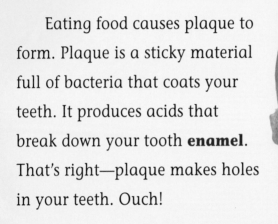

Eating food causes plaque to form. Plaque is a sticky material full of bacteria that coats your teeth. It produces acids that break down your tooth **enamel**. That's right—plaque makes holes in your teeth. Ouch!

Ewww Fact!

Before toothpaste was invented, people used ground-up chalk or ashes from a fire to clean their teeth.

enamel—the hard outer surface of the teeth

DON'T SHARE AMOEBAS

Brushing helps remove quivering masses of microscopic goo hiding between your teeth. No, not your leftover breakfast. They're teeth **amoebas**. These tiny creatures live off bits of food stuck in the crevices of your teeth. You can get these relatively harmless microbes by kissing or sharing cups with people—any time you share saliva. You can also get them from sharing saliva with your pet!

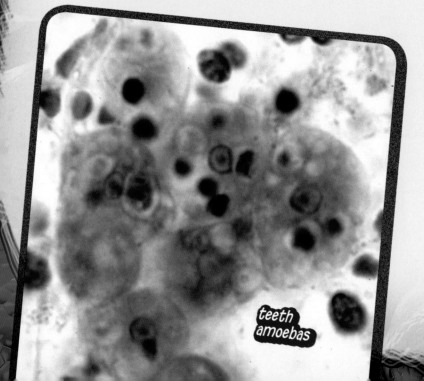

teeth amoebas

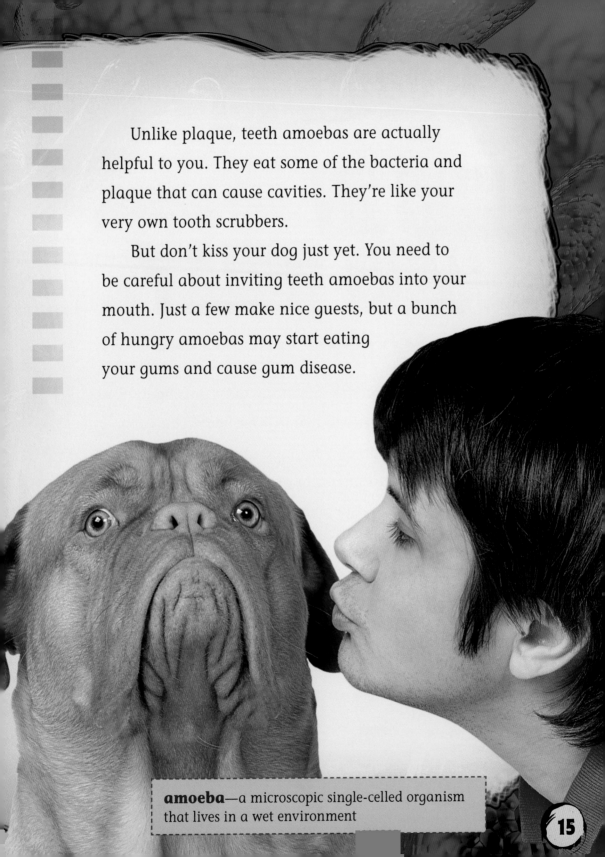

Unlike plaque, teeth amoebas are actually helpful to you. They eat some of the bacteria and plaque that can cause cavities. They're like your very own tooth scrubbers.

But don't kiss your dog just yet. You need to be careful about inviting teeth amoebas into your mouth. Just a few make nice guests, but a bunch of hungry amoebas may start eating your gums and cause gum disease.

amoeba—a microscopic single-celled organism that lives in a wet environment

Chapter 3

BUGS IN YOUR BELLY

Your stomach is one of the most unfriendly places for a critter to live in your body. The harsh acids used to break your food apart make it a difficult environment for organisms. Only the strong survive—and some microbes are very strong.

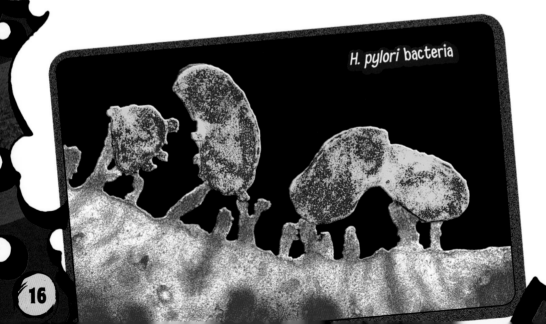

H. pylori bacteria

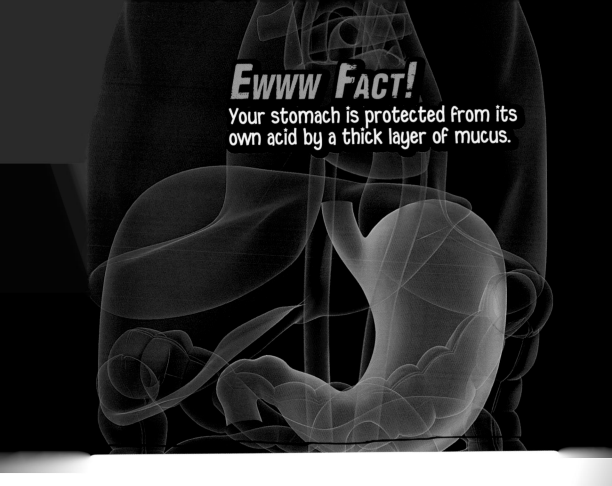

One microbe that can handle the high acid levels is *H. pylori*. Between 40 and 50 percent of people have this bacterium in their stomachs. *H. pylori* survives the really strong acids by burrowing into the lining of the stomach. Then it releases a substance that reduces the acid level. It gets comfy and can live there throughout a person's life.

Normally, *H. pylori* is harmless. But sometimes it can cause ulcers, which are breaks in the stomach tissue.

HELPFUL MICROBES

From the stomach, let's head into the twisting, turning tube of your intestines. Trillions of intestinal microbes live here. You may not like the idea of creepy crawlies inside you. But without some of them, you'd be in trouble.

Probiotics keep your stomach working normally. These are good bacteria found in both your stomach and intestines. They help break down food and allow the intestines to absorb the nutrients we need to stay healthy. Probiotics also help keep harmful bacteria from multiplying too much.

probiotic bacteria

probiotic—a type of bacterium that helps people stay healthy

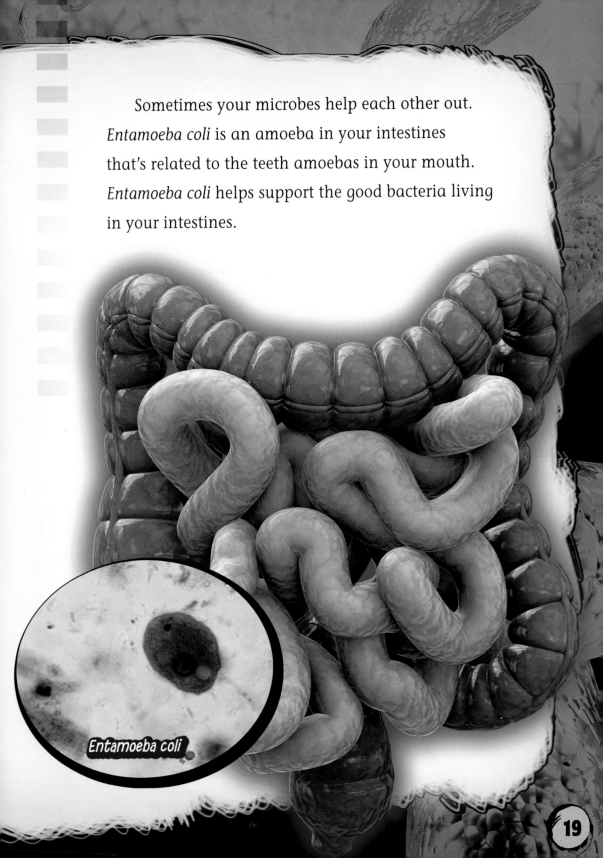

Sometimes your microbes help each other out.
Entamoeba coli is an amoeba in your intestines
that's related to the teeth amoebas in your mouth.
Entamoeba coli helps support the good bacteria living
in your intestines.

Entamoeba coli

DOUBLE IDENTITY

Escherichia coli, or *E. coli*, is another bacterium found in your intestines. Normally, people fear these bacteria because they can cause severe diarrhea and even death. But some types of *E. coli* live peacefully in your intestines. They are harmless and actually help your body make and absorb vitamins.

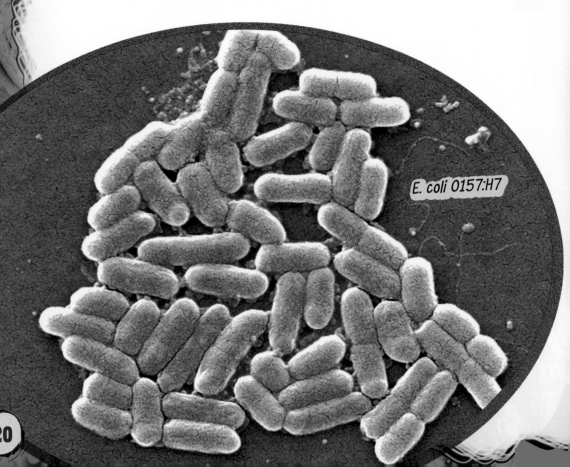

E. coli 0157:H7

E. coli O157:H7 is the bad type that people worry about. It can be found in undercooked food or **contaminated** water. If you eat these bacteria, you will get very sick. Always order your hamburgers and other meat "well done" to make sure they're cooked enough to be safe.

Ewww Fact!

More than 500 different kinds of bacteria live in your stomach and intestines. Their total weight can be up to 3.3 pounds (1.5 kilograms)!

contaminated—unfit for use because of contact with a harmful substance

WORMS

Have you ever eaten a worm? Not the pink earthworms that come out when it rains. We're talking about roundworms. You can get these microscopic parasites from eating contaminated meat that has not been properly cooked. Impossible to see, roundworms are only 0.04 inch (1 mm) in length. But once inside your intestines, they can grow as long as a ruler!

Roundworms feast on body fluids and tiny food particles floating by. But these worms are not good guests. Roundworms can cause stomach pain, coughing, rashes, and weight loss.

To avoid getting worms, wash your hands before and after handling uncooked food. And be sure your food is cooked completely before you eat it.

Ewww Fact!
More than 100 roundworms can infect your intestines at one time.

roundworm under a microscope

roundworms

Chapter 4

FUNKY FEET

Last but not least, take a look at your feet. One whiff of your sneakers will tell you that feet can stink. Your feet contain more than 250,000 sweat glands. They are the sweatiest parts of your body.

But sweat is only part of the problem. The nasty smell is caused by bacteria that eat your sweat.

Ewww Fact!
In one day each foot can produce more than 1 pint (0.5 liter) of sweat!

UNFRIENDLY FOOT FUNGUS

Bacteria might not be the only organisms living on your feet. Some people get a **fungus** called athlete's foot. You don't have to be athletic to get it. This itchy problem can be found around anyone's sweaty toes.

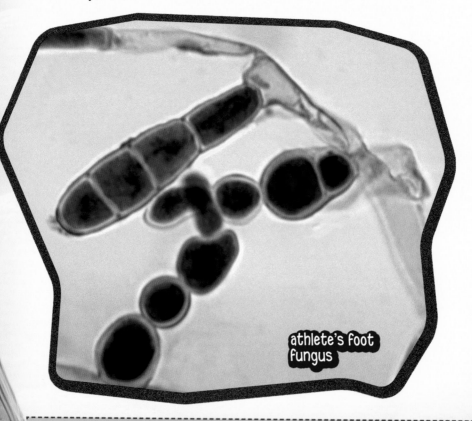

athlete's foot fungus

fungus—a single-celled organism that lives by breaking down and absorbing the natural material it lives in

decomposer—an organism that lives off dead or decaying matter

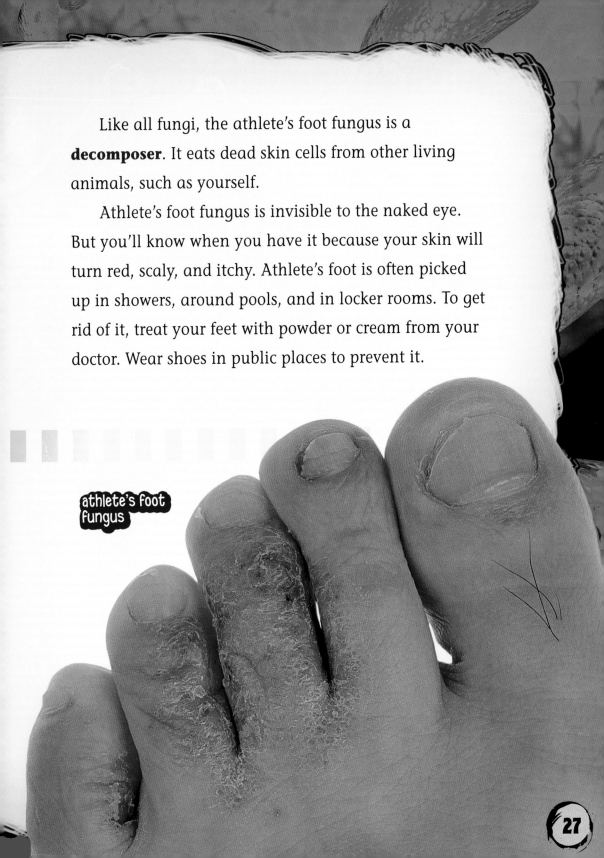

Like all fungi, the athlete's foot fungus is a **decomposer**. It eats dead skin cells from other living animals, such as yourself.

Athlete's foot fungus is invisible to the naked eye. But you'll know when you have it because your skin will turn red, scaly, and itchy. Athlete's foot is often picked up in showers, around pools, and in locker rooms. To get rid of it, treat your feet with powder or cream from your doctor. Wear shoes in public places to prevent it.

athlete's foot fungus

LIVING WITH MICROBES

Let's face it, everyone has bugs. You have your your own special set, different from anyone else's. Even boys and girls have different types of microbes living on them.

You can't avoid all the harmful microbes out there. However, a healthy immune system will help you fight them. Your immune system defends your body against invaders.

How do you keep your immune system strong? You can start by eating a healthy diet and getting plenty of rest. And remember to wash your hands often. Keeping unfriendly microbes off your skin is a good first step to keeping harmful germs out of your body.

Hand Sanitizer

Glossary

amoeba (uh-MEE-buh)—a microscopic single-celled organism that lives in a wet environment

contaminated (kuhn-TA-muh-nay-tuhd)—unfit for use because of contact with a harmful substance

decomposer (dee-kuhm-PO-zur)—an organism that lives off dead or decaying matter

enamel (i-NAM-uhl)—the hard outer surface of the teeth

fungus (FUHN-guhs)—a single-celled organism that lives by breaking down and absorbing the natural material it lives in

microbe (MYE-krobe)—a living thing that is too small to see without a microscope

organism (OR-guh-niz-uhm)—a living thing such as a plant, animal, bacterium, or fungus

parasite (PAIR-uh-site)—a small organism that lives on or inside a person or animal and causes harm

probiotic (pro-bye-AH-tik)—a type of bacterium that lives in the stomach and intestines and helps people stay healthy

virus (VYE-russ)—a germ that copies itself inside the body's cells

Read More

Macaulay, David. *The Way We Work: Getting to Know the Amazing Human Body.* Boston: Houghton Mifflin, 2008.

Perritano, John. *Bugs on Your Body: Nature's Creepiest Creatures Live on You!* Current Science. Pleasantville, N.Y.: Gareth Stevens Pub., 2010.

Perritano, John. *Bugs That Live On Us.* Bug Alert. New York: Marshall Cavendish Benchmark, 2009.

Internet Sites

FactHound offers a safe, fun way to find Internet sites related to this book. All of the sites on FactHound have been researched by our staff.

Here's all you do:

Visit *www.facthound.com*

Type in this code: 9781429665308

Check out projects, games and lots more at
www.capstonekids.com

Index